Exploring Volcanic Activity

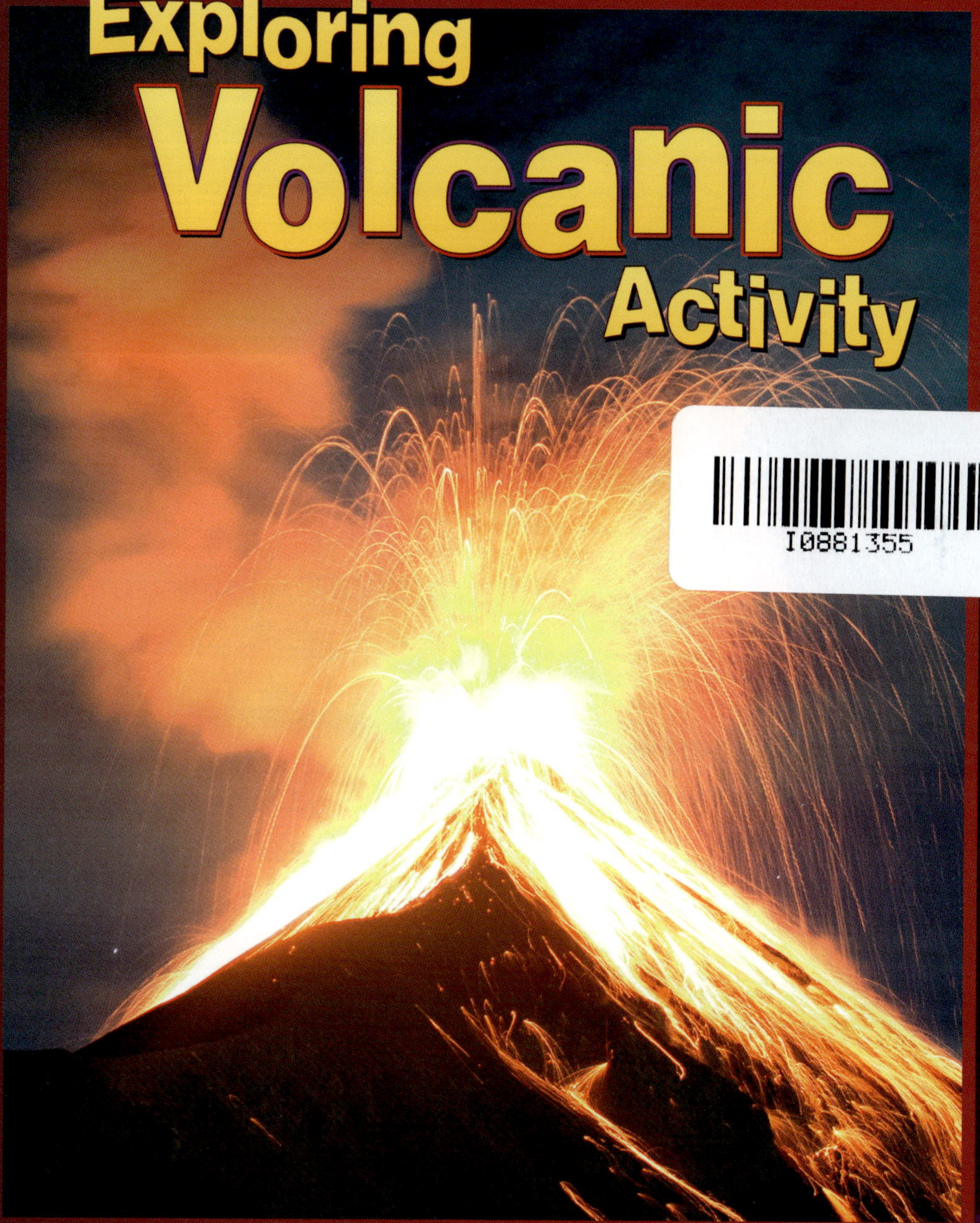

Nick Cimarusti, M.S.

Smithsonian

Contributing Author

Heather Schultz, M.A.

Consultants

Liz Cottrell
Research Geologist, Department of Mineral Science
National Museum of Natural History

Tamieka Grizzle, Ed.D.
K–5 STEM Lab Instructor
Harmony Leland Elementary School

Stephanie Anastasopoulos, M.Ed.
TOSA, STREAM Integration
Solana Beach School District

Publishing Credits

Rachelle Cracchiolo, M.S.Ed., *Publisher*
Conni Medina, M.A.Ed., *Managing Editor*
Diana Kenney, M.A.Ed., NBCT, *Series Developer*
Véronique Bos, *Creative Director*
June Kikuchi, *Content Director*
Robin Erickson, *Art Director*
Seth Rogers, *Editor*
Mindy Duits, *Senior Graphic Designer*
Smithsonian Science Education Center

Image Credits: pp.2–3 © Smithsonian; p.4 Peter V. Bianchi/National Geographic/Getty Images; p.7, 14 (bottom) NASA; p.10 (left) Louise Gubb/ Corbis via Getty Images; p.13 USGS; p.16 Dana Stephenson//Getty Images; p.17 (bottom left) Douglas Peebles/Science Source; p.19 (bottom) NOAA/ NASA; p.21 Corbis via Getty Images; p.22 (left) Julia Kuznetsova/Dreamstime; p.23 Nature Picture Library/Alamy; p.24 Monica Schroeder/Science Source; p.25 NOAA; p.27 Hemis/Alamy; p.32 (right) Manfred Thuerig/Dreamstime; all other images from iStock and/or Shutterstock.

Library of Congress Cataloging-in-Publication Data

Names: Cimarusti, Nick, author.
Title: Exploring volcanic activity / Nick Cimarusti.
Description: Huntington Beach, CA : Teacher Created Materials, [2019] | Audience: Grade 4 to 6. | Includes index. |
Identifiers: LCCN 2018005460 (print) | LCCN 2018023173 (ebook) | ISBN 9781493869435 (E-book) | ISBN 9781493867035 (pbk.)
Subjects: LCSH: Volcanoes--Juvenile literature.
Classification: LCC QE521.3 (ebook) | LCC QE521.3 .C55 2019 (print) | DDC 551.21--dc23
LC record available at https://lccn.loc.gov/2018005460

Smithsonian

Teacher Created Materials

5301 Oceanus Drive
Huntington Beach, CA 92649-1030
www.tcmpub.com

ISBN 978-1-4938-6703-5

Printed by: 590835
Printed in: Taiwan

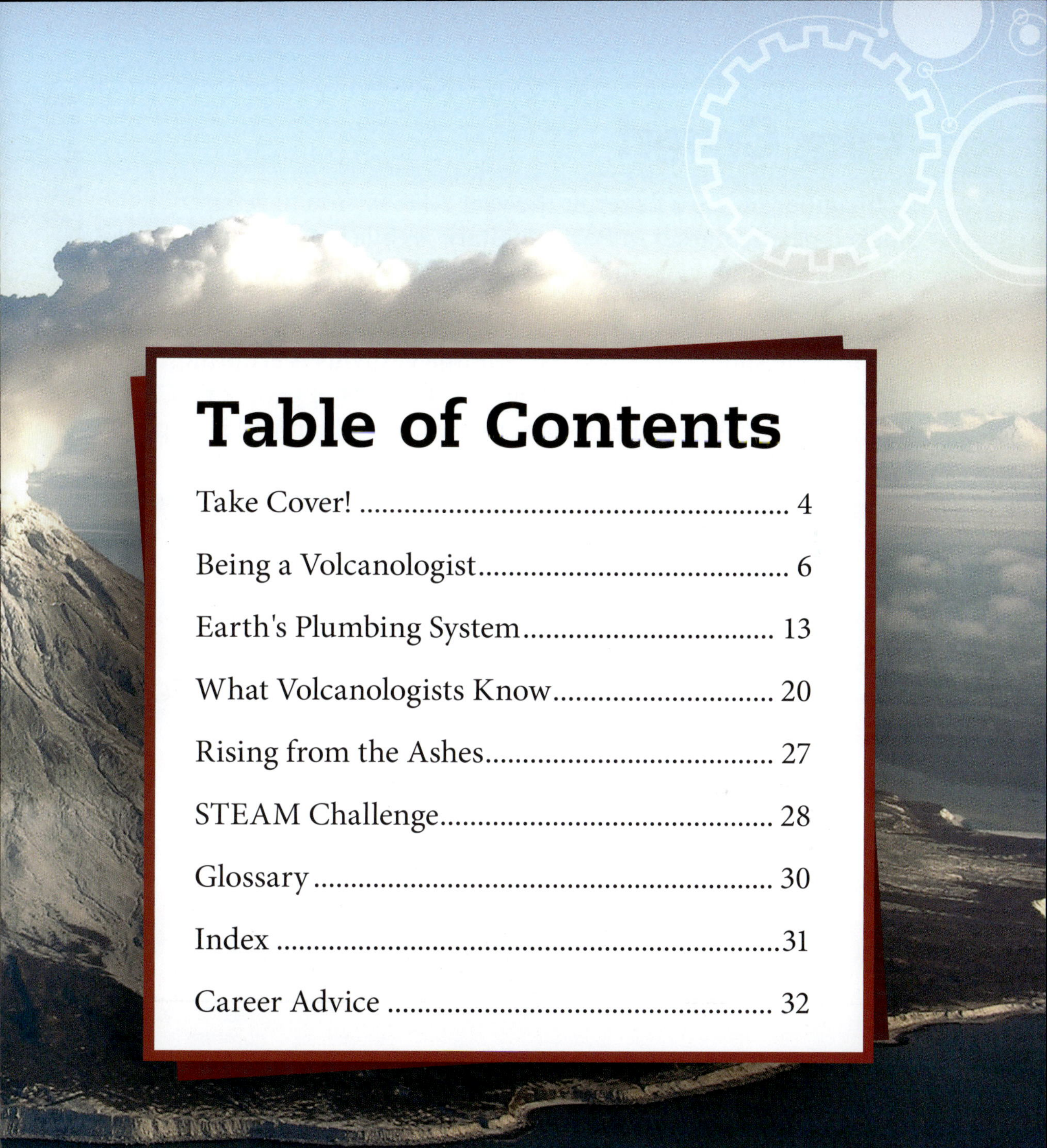

Table of Contents

Take Cover!

Imagine you are a fisher in the year AD 79. You have just docked near a market in Pompeii, Italy. While your crew unloads the ship, you enjoy the sea breeze. Suddenly, you hear shouts from the streets. Black clouds fill the sky.

Someone shouts as they pass, "Mount Vesuvius is erupting!" Mount Vesuvius is the nearby volcano. Crowds of people run for their lives. **Ash** makes it hard to breathe. When will it stop?

This 1961 painting shows people fleeing Mt. Vesuvius's eruption.

What Is a Volcano?

Disasters such as Vesuvius inspire scientists to study volcanoes. Volcanoes may seem like they won't affect you, but people all over the world live near active volcanoes. Active volcanoes are those that have erupted in the last 10,000 years.

Volcanoes come in different shapes and sizes. Scientists can learn a lot about the planet by studying volcanoes. They are like windows into Earth. They help scientists see what is inside.

Scientists who study volcanoes have a special title. They are called volcanologists (vohl-kuh-NAH-luh-jists). They travel to volcanoes to learn from them. They try to figure out how volcanoes work and where they occur.

Mount Vesuvius is still active! It last erupted in 1944.

Being a Volcanologist

Earth has a long history. Volcanoes are a big part of that past. They leave clues, such as gases and rocks. Volcanologists study these clues. They can learn a lot from volcanoes. They can learn about Earth's past. They can learn about **geology**, too. Volcanoes are geology in action.

Volcanologists have exciting jobs. They travel all over the world to study volcanoes. Sometimes, they ride in helicopters to get to the top of volcanoes. They may travel to volcanic islands. Once there, they may have to do a lot of hiking up mountains and hills. When they reach their destinations, they dig for samples. They take notes of what they see. Then, they go home and record their data. They can share it with other volcanologists. The data they gather are like tiny time capsules from the earth.

Volcanologists collect samples.

ARTS

Dark Inspiration

Volcanologists are not the only people inspired by volcanic activity. In 1815, Mount Tambora in Indonesia erupted. This volcano changed the whole planet. Ash clouds covered the sky for more than a year. Crops froze and died. Heavy rain caused floods. Nights seemed darker than normal. One dark, stormy night in Switzerland, author Mary Shelley was inspired. Shelley told her friends a scary story about life and death. They were terrified! That story became the novel *Frankenstein*.

Blazing the Trail

The Global Volcanism Program (GVP) is made up of a group of volcanologists. The goal of the program is to record volcanic activity on Earth.

The GVP records and shares data from all over the world. Since its founding, the GVP has shared thousands of reports. The GVP also stores all of their volcanic activity reports in an **archive**. That will help future volcanologists.

A fountain of lava erupts from one of the Kamchatka volcanoes in Russia.

Asking Questions

The GVP has learned a lot from studying volcanoes. They learned that big eruptions happen when volcanoes have not erupted for thousands of years. They also learned about the **frequency** of eruptions. They found that small eruptions happen more often than big eruptions. The GVP learned these things by asking questions and working to find answers.

Volcanoes change the surface of Earth. These changes are measured. Samples of rock and ash are collected. Volcanologists test the samples for **composition**. They want to know what is in a sample of ash.

crater of a volcano

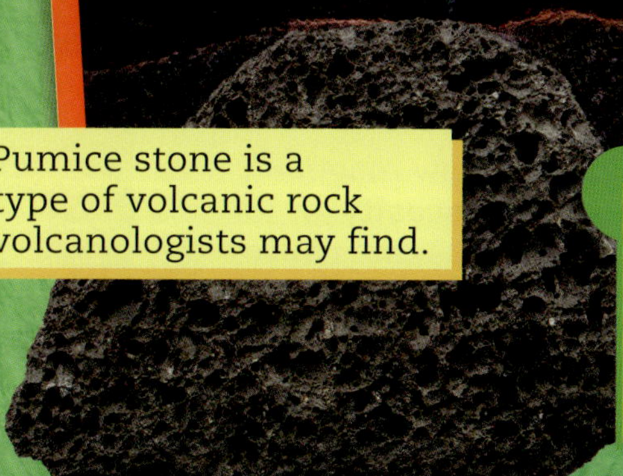

Pumice stone is a type of volcanic rock volcanologists may find.

The word *volcano* comes from *Vulcan*, the name of the Roman god of fire. But, even though volcanoes look like they are releasing flames, volcanoes are never on fire.

Volcanologists try to visit every volcano. But going to an erupting volcano is not safe! This is why records are useful. The GVP database is full of historical records.

Volcanologists use historical records to learn about dangerous volcanoes. Past eruptions teach them about volcanoes today. They can answer questions about an eruption, such as "How long did it last?," "What came out?," and "Who was affected?"

SCIENCE

Hot Stuff!

Magma is molten rock. *Molten* means the rock is so hot that it is liquid. Three factors change how magma behaves. They are temperature, gas, and **viscosity**, or its thickness or stickiness. Different types of magma cause different types of eruptions. Viscous magma is explosive. This is because gases get trapped and pressure builds. When magma reaches Earth's surface, it is called lava.

Volcanoes that show no signs of erupting are safer to visit. Scientists can get close to collect rocks to study. Each rock is different. Some volcanic rocks are tiny. Other rocks are big boulders. Some have holes all over them! These samples tell scientists stories. They can see where the rocks came from inside Earth. They can also learn how they got to the surface.

This volcano is located in Africa.

Lots and Lots of Data

The GVP has an online database to collect facts about volcanoes. Databases organize a lot of information. They are also easy to use. Each eruption from history has its own profile. The profile lists the location of the volcano and other facts. The GVP shares this data. The U.S. government, NASA, and websites like Google Earth™ use the GVP database. New data is added every week.

Each eruption gets a number. The number describes the size of the eruption. The scale is from 0 to 9. This helps people compare eruptions through time. A volcano in the United States once scored a 5! It was Mount St. Helens in Washington.

Mount St. Helens erupting

Earth's Plumbing System

Volcanoes are like Earth's plumbing system. Only the top part of a volcano is visible. Think of a kitchen sink. You only see the faucet. But it is connected to pipes that are hidden under the sink. The pipes direct the water. They control how hot water gets. Magma can be found under the surface, like pipes under a sink.

Yellowstone National Park is located above an ancient supervolcano. It last erupted about 630,000 years ago.

Volcanologists study Earth closely. They know it inside and out! Earth has four layers. The top layer is called the crust. The crust is broken into huge, solid pieces. They are called **tectonic plates**. Tectonic plates are like puzzle pieces.

Below the crust is the mantle. The mantle is a mixture of liquid rock and solid rock. Under the mantle is the liquid outer core. Beneath the outer core is the solid inner core. Scientists know about the layers because they study energy waves. They measure how energy waves travel through Earth.

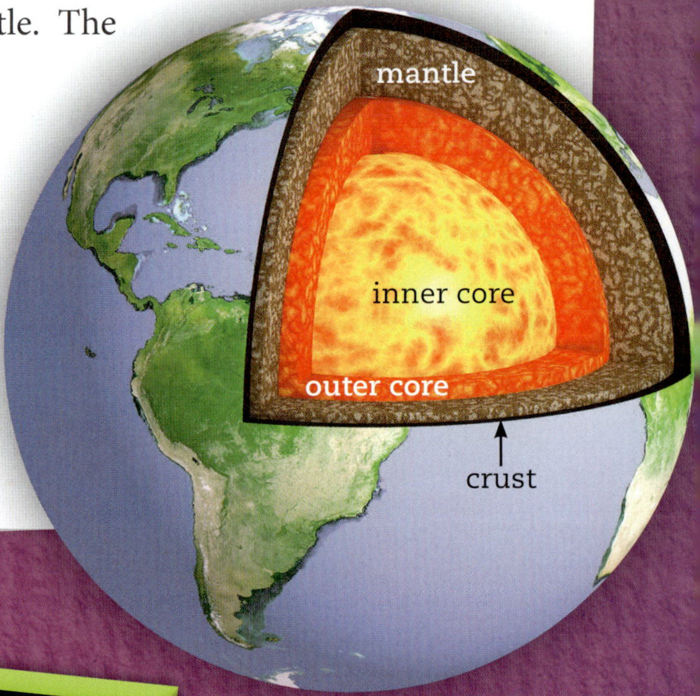

ENGINEERING

Volcano Robots

Scientists want to see inside volcanoes, but temperatures are too high! That is why they invented volcano robots. These small robots can enter volcanoes when humans cannot. Two wheels let the robots zip right in! Scientists control the robots from a safe distance. The robots have cameras that take video footage and photos. They also take measurements and draw maps.

Feel the Earth Move

Why do volcanoes erupt in the first place? Scientists believe **convection** is the answer. Convection gets the layers of Earth moving.

Under the crust, the mantle is always moving in large circles. This movement causes the tectonic plates above to move, too. As plates move, magma rises through openings in the crust. Volcanoes form.

The areas where plates meet are called tectonic plate boundaries. Some plates are pushed together. Other plates pull away from each other. And some plates slide under other plates. Boundaries are also at the bottom of the ocean. In fact, most volcanoes are underwater!

Earth's Major Tectonic Plates

Volcanoes can be found where plates meet (red lines).

Australia has very few active volcanoes because it rests in the middle of a tectonic plate.

Sizzling Structures

Volcanoes have different shapes. But they all function the same. Over time, hard lava and rocks pile up near the opening to a bigger tunnel, called the central **vent**. Central vents go far underground. They lead to **magma chambers**.

Each volcano is unique. But volcanologists try to organize volcanoes into groups. The shape of the volcano results from its eruptions. Cinder cone volcanoes are the simplest. They often only erupt once. Shield volcanoes are short but wide. Their lava usually flows out like syrup, not in big explosions.

Composite volcanoes are large, cone-shaped volcanoes. These volcanoes are among the tallest. They can be more than 2,400 meters (8,000 feet) tall! Their magma is very explosive. They do not erupt a lot, but their eruptions are the most dangerous.

Parts of a Volcano

a composite volcano in Mt. Cotopaxi, Ecuador

a cinder cone volcano in Bartolome Island, Ecuador

a shield volcano in Hawai'i, United States

Now the action starts! Eruptions can be violent. Other times, lava slowly pours out. Lava can even move slower than a person running! Eruptions can last for minutes or days. Some volcanoes erupt for years. There are names for all types of eruptions.

Volcanoes in Hawai'i have calm and slow eruptions. But lava can also shoot out in short spurts. This is called a fire fountain, even though nothing is on fire.

Plinian eruptions create a lot of damage. They make huge clouds of ash and **pyroclastic flows**. These are like avalanches of rock, ash, and hot gas.

Whatever the type, all volcanic eruptions produce lava and gas. They can also make **pyroclastic** rock. This mixture then explodes into **fragments**. Ash from the eruptions is actually powdered rock, not smoke!

lava flow

pyroclastic flow

Vulcanian eruption

Strombolian eruption

MATHEMATICS

Eye in the Sky

Volcanologists take a lot of measurements. Even small changes are important. Satellites can track changes too small for people to see. Sometimes, the ground inflates before an eruption. It puffs up because magma is moving to the surface. Satellites alert volcanologists when this happens. Satellites also make it easier to keep track of more volcanoes. With satellites, every volcano can be watched.

What Volcanologists Know

It is hard to predict eruptions. Scientists look for warning signs. One major sign is when small earthquakes happen near a volcano. Moving magma causes the ground to shake. Satellites also look for changes. They monitor volcanoes from space. They can see even the smallest movement.

One day, volcanologists hope to **forecast** eruptions. Then, people who live near volcanoes would have warning. They could prepare better and leave if they have to. But people at GVP want to predict more. How long will an eruption last? How dangerous will it be?

Types of Gases

Forecasting eruptions could save a lot of lives. In the meantime, scientists use what they know about chemistry to better understand volcanoes.

Scientists know that volcanoes are filled with gases. Water vapor is the most common gas from volcanoes. But other gases, such as carbon dioxide and sulfur dioxide, are also present. When released, these gases can react with the air. The combinations can be deadly!

Volcanologists use a tool called a thermocouple to measure a volcano's temperature. Glass thermometers would just melt!

Two geologists measure the skylight of a lava tube in Hawai'i.

Volcanologists already know that gases come out of magma. Now, they want to understand how these mixtures work. The types of gases in magma lead to different types of eruptions. They might be explosive. Or lava might pour out slowly.

Scientists collect gases in bottles. They also use sensors to measure gas levels. In addition to gases, scientists collect ash and rocks. They use all the samples they collect to better understand volcanoes.

volcanic eruption in Iceland

Iceland is almost completely made of volcanic rocks.

Air It Out

Take a deep breath. The gases you just inhaled came from volcanoes. All the gases we breathe first came from inside the planet. Humans get most of the oxygen we breathe today from plants. But before plants existed, volcanoes created the atmosphere. Eruptions pushed many gases to the surface. The gases then mixed together to create the air.

Carbon dioxide is another gas that is released by eruptions. This gas can cause the **greenhouse effect**. This happens when a pollutant, such as carbon dioxide, becomes trapped in the atmosphere and sends heat back to Earth.

TECHNOLOGY

Breaking the Ice

Energy sources can be harmful. Some are not "clean." But Iceland might have a solution. Scientists in Iceland have drilled into a volcano. They want to use geothermal energy. *Geothermal* means "heat from the earth." The drilled holes cause hot steam to rise up from the volcano. The steam powers a machine to create electricity. This idea is not expensive, and it creates a lot of energy.

Volcanic Creations

Volcanologists also know that volcanoes are responsible for forming new crust. New crust is formed at tectonic plate boundaries in the oceans. Eruptions push out magma, which then cools into crust.

Volcanoes are the reason we have land to walk on. But with all this new crust being formed, why doesn't Earth grow bigger and bigger?

A process called **subduction** prevents the planet from growing too large. Subduction pushes extra crust under old crust. The extra crust returns to the hot mantle and melts.

Continental Plate Subduction

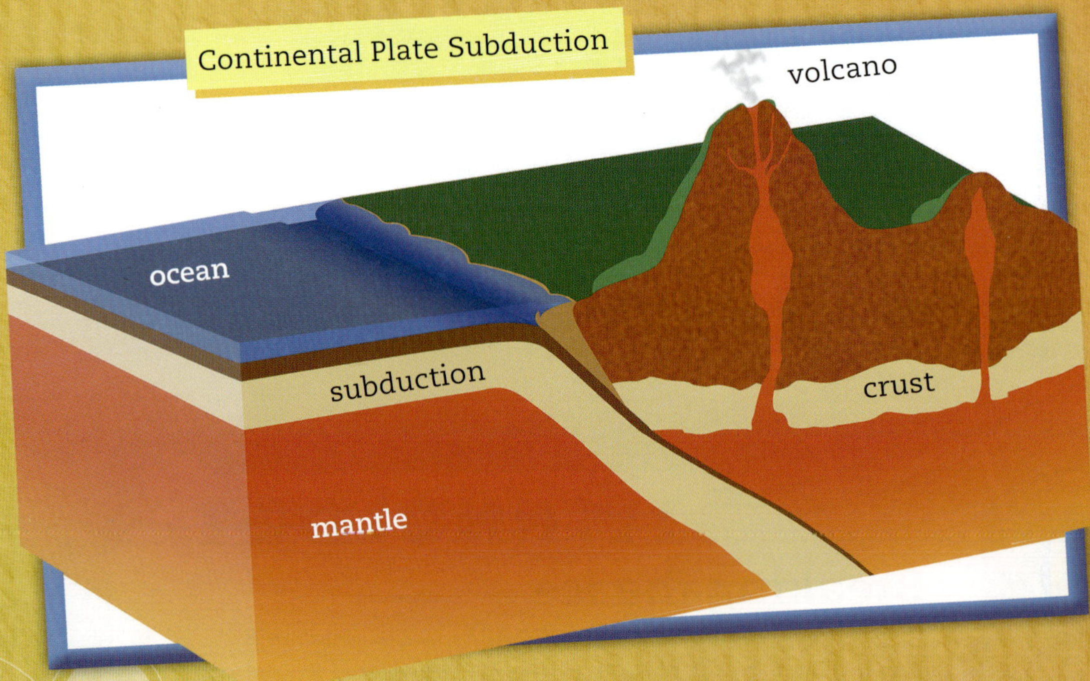

Volcanoes are also the reason we have oceans. Water vapor erupted from the first volcanoes. Later, the planet cooled. Water vapor fell as rain. The rain then gathered into the oceans. All this happened thanks to volcanoes!

An underwater volcano erupts, sending ash into the air.

Chimneys in an ocean release liquids heated by magma.

ruins at Pompeii

body at Pompeii

Rising from the Ashes

The ruins from Pompeii are a powerful sight. Lonely stone pillars are scattered in groups. Bodies covered in dried volcanic mud are frozen in time. It looks as though nothing has changed in the years since they lived and breathed.

Mount Vesuvius is an example of the scary power of volcanoes. Yet without volcanoes, there would be no oxygen to breathe. There would be no land to walk on. There would be no oceans to swim in.

Volcanologists all over the world work together through groups such as the GVP. These groups will continue to learn, discover, and teach. Thanks to them, we know more about the planet's past. And as a result, we know more about Earth's future.

Volcanologists record the location of a volcano.

STEAM CHALLENGE

Define the Problem

Volcanologists from the GVP are still developing methods to better understand volcanoes. In the meantime, how can we make living near an active volcano safer? Your task is to design and build a structure that will keep a cotton ball safe in a model volcanic eruption.

Constraints: Your structure must be made using only paper.

Criteria: Your paper structure must prevent lava from touching a cotton ball.

Research and Brainstorm

What are the dangers of living near a volcano? How can you keep people safe? Will you use materials that can withstand the lava or will it alter the flow of lava?

Design and Build

After making a list of different possibilities, decide which safety measure(s) you will take. Sketch your design, and build a model to test your solutions.

Test and Improve

Place your structure about 15 centimeters (6 inches) away from a model volcano and then make it erupt. How far did the lava flow? What items did the lava reach? Did your cotton ball stay untouched by lava? What improvements can you make? Modify your design and try again.

Reflect and Share

How would different types of volcanic eruptions affect your design? Do you think your design could protect from a volcanic eruption? How could your design be improved?

Glossary

archive—a place for storing information

ash—fine rock powder

composition—what an object is made of

convection—movement in a gas or liquid in which the warmer parts move up and the colder parts move down

forecast—to calculate or predict based on the study of available data

fragments—small pieces

frequency—how often an event happens

geology—the study of Earth and its history

greenhouse effect—the warming of Earth's atmosphere, which is caused by air pollution

magma chambers—where volcanoes store magma before eruption

pyroclastic—made of rock, gas, and magma ejected from a volcano

pyroclastic flows—avalanches of hot gases and lava

subduction—the recycling of Earth's crust

tectonic plates—solid pieces of Earth's crust

vent—an opening for the escape of gas or liquid or for the release of pressure

viscosity—the thickness or stickiness of a liquid

Index

CAREER ADVICE
from Smithsonian

Do you want to be a volcanologist?
Here are some tips to get you started.

"I've loved science since I was a little kid. I did science experiments with my dad. You don't need to be the top mathematician in your school to have a career in science. Instead, you need to be able to work in a team, communicate, and tell people your ideas. Find what you love. Then, find mentors who can teach you everything they know. Before you know it, you will become the teacher for future generations."—*Liz Cottrell, Geologist*

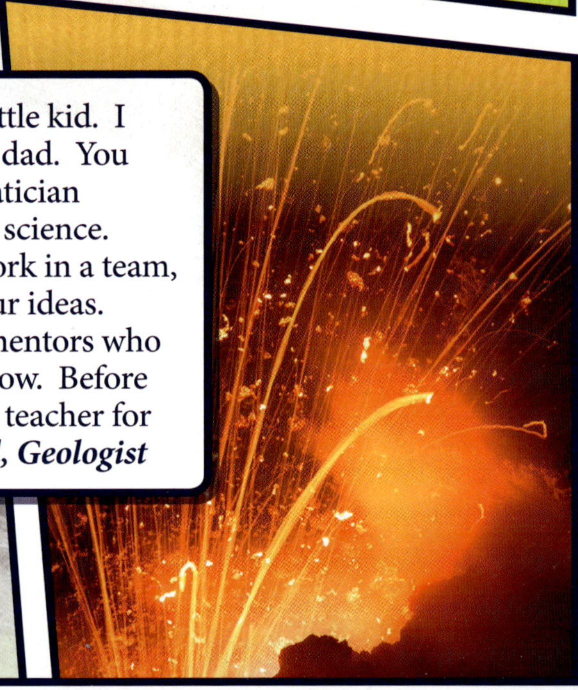

"I wanted to become a scientist because I love science and playing outdoors. Today, I am a geologist who studies volcanoes. I visit volcanoes and observe their eruptions from a safe distance. I use video and temperature cameras to record what is happening. You need to understand earthquakes and geology, as well as computers, to simulate a volcano safely in a lab." —*Ben Andrews, Geologist*